Daily Love Quotes: 365 days of Inspiration and Motivation

By Daniel Willey

I'm sending this through Cupcake. Thanks for waiting bro. Enjoy! C.B.

ISBN-13: 978-1494913632
ISBN-10: 1494913631

All rights reserved.
Published by Easy Publishing Company
http://www.easypublishingcompany.com
contact@easypublishingcompany.com
Salt Lake City, UT 84108

First Edition: December 2013
Printed in the United States of America

Table of Contents

Ways to Use this Book:

1. Start your day by reading a quote. Start at number 1 and read one quote per day. Write the quote down and share it throughout your day with others.
2. Buy a journal and record your responses to each of the quotes. Write down your feelings, thoughts, and inspirations.
3. Read this book as you would read any other book, from beginning to end.
4. Pick a random number, 1-365, then find and read that quote. Use it on days or at times when you need extra inspiration.

Introduction

I have always considered quotes to be a very valuable asset to my inspiration. For years I have scoured the web to find meaningful quotes from inspirational people. When I find an especially meaningful quote, I love to share it with those close to me. I think that when you share something special to yourself, it can become even more meaningful and help out others.

NOTE: The Quotes in this book are collected from many sources and time periods. To respect the integrity of the authors' work, I have made every reasonable effort to correctly attribute each quote to the original author, but in a few cases it was impossible to find the exact original quote. I have made every effort to give credit to the person who first spoke the classic version of each quote.

1

"I'm selfish, impatient and a little insecure. I make mistakes, I am out of control and at times hard to handle. But if you can't handle me at my worst, then you sure as hell don't deserve me at my best."
— Marilyn Monroe

2

"You've gotta dance like there's nobody watching,
Love like you'll never be hurt,
Sing like there's nobody listening,
And live like it's heaven on earth."
— William W. Purkey

3

"You know you're in love when you can't fall asleep because reality is finally better than your dreams."

— Dr. Seuss

4

"A friend is someone who knows all
about you and still loves you."
— Elbert Hubbard

5

"Darkness cannot drive out darkness:
only light can do that. Hate cannot
drive out hate: only love can do that."
— Martin Luther King Jr., A Testament
of Hope: The Essential Writings and
Speeches

6

"It is better to be hated for what you
are than to be loved for what you are
not."
— André Gide, Autumn Leaves

7

"Only once in your life, I truly believe, you find someone who can completely turn your world around. You tell them things that you've never shared with another soul and they absorb everything you say and actually want to hear more. You share hopes for the future, dreams that will never come true, goals that were never achieved and the many disappointments life has thrown at you. When something wonderful happens, you can't wait to tell them about it, knowing they will share in your excitement. They are not embarrassed to cry with you when you are hurting or laugh with you when you make a fool of yourself. Never do they hurt your feelings or make you feel like you are not good enough, but rather they build you up and show you the things about yourself that make you special and even beautiful. There is never any pressure, jealousy or competition but only a quiet calmness when they are around. You can be yourself and not worry about what they will think of you because they love you for who you are. The things that seem insignificant to most people such as a note, song or walk become invaluable treasures kept safe in your heart to cherish forever. Memories of your childhood come back and are so clear and vivid it's like being young again. Colours seem brighter and more brilliant. Laughter seems part of daily life where before it was infrequent or didn't exist at all. A phone call or two during the day helps to get you through a long day's work and always brings a smile to your face. In their presence, there's no need for continuous conversation, but you find you're quite content in just having them nearby. Things that never interested you before become fascinating because you know they are important to this person who is so special to you. You think of this person on every occasion and in everything you do. Simple things bring them to mind like a pale blue sky, gentle wind or even a storm cloud on the horizon. You open your heart knowing that there's a chance it may be broken one day and in opening your heart, you experience a love and joy that you never dreamed possible. You find that being vulnerable is the only way to allow your heart to feel true pleasure that's so real it scares you. You find strength in knowing you have a true friend and possibly a soul mate who will remain loyal to the end. Life seems completely different, exciting

and worthwhile. Your only hope and security is in knowing that they are a part of your life."
— Bob Marley

8

"We accept the love we think we deserve."
— Stephen Chbosky, The Perks of Being a Wallflower

9

"The opposite of love is not hate, it's indifference. The opposite of art is not ugliness, it's indifference. The opposite of faith is not heresy, it's indifference. And the opposite of life is not death, it's indifference."
— Elie Wiesel

10

"It is not a lack of love, but a lack of friendship that makes unhappy marriages."
— Friedrich Nietzsche

11
"There is never a time or place for true love. It happens accidentally, in a heartbeat, in a single flashing, throbbing moment."
— Sarah Dessen, The Truth About Forever

12
"I love you without knowing how, or when, or from where. I love you simply, without problems or pride: I love you in this way because I do not know any other way of loving but this, in which there is no I or you, so intimate that your hand upon my

chest is my hand, so intimate that when I fall asleep your eyes close."
— Pablo Neruda, 100 Love Sonnets

13
"Have you ever been in love? Horrible isn't it? It makes you so vulnerable. It opens your chest and it opens up your heart and it means that someone can get inside you and mess you up."
— Neil Gaiman, The Sandman, Vol. 9: The Kindly Ones

14
"Love all, trust a few, do wrong to none."
— William Shakespeare, All's Well That Ends Well

15
"This life is what you make it. No matter what, you're going to mess up

sometimes, it's a universal truth. But the good part is you get to decide how you're going to mess it up. Girls will be your friends - they'll act like it anyway. But just remember, some come, some go. The ones that stay with you through everything - they're your true best friends. Don't let go of them. Also remember, sisters make the best friends in the world. As for lovers, well, they'll come and go too. And baby, I hate to say it, most of them - actually pretty much all of them are going to break your heart, but you can't give up because if you give up, you'll never find your soulmate. You'll never find that half who makes you whole and that goes for everything. Just because you fail once, doesn't mean you're gonna fail at everything. Keep trying, hold on, and always, always, always believe in yourself,

because if you don't, then who will, sweetie? So keep your head high, keep your chin up, and most importantly, keep smiling, because life's a beautiful thing and there's so much to smile about."
— Marilyn Monroe

16

"Being deeply loved by someone gives you strength, while loving someone deeply gives you courage."
— Lao Tzu

17

"As he read, I fell in love the way you fall asleep: slowly, and then all at once."
— John Green, The Fault in Our Stars

18

"Love is that condition in which the happiness of another person is essential to your own."
— Robert A. Heinlein, Stranger in a Strange Land

19

"I am nothing special, of this I am sure. I am a common man with common thoughts and I've led a common life. There are no monuments dedicated to me and my name will soon be forgotten, but I've loved another with all my heart and soul, and to me, this has always been enough.."
— Nicholas Sparks, The Notebook

20

"You may not be her first, her last, or her only. She loved before she may love again. But if she loves you now,

what else matters? She's not perfect - you aren't either, and the two of you may never be perfect together but if she can make you laugh, cause you to think twice, and admit to being human and making mistakes, hold onto her and give her the most you can. She may not be thinking about you every second of the day, but she will give you a part of her that she knows you can break - her heart. So don't hurt her, don't change her, don't analyze and don't expect more than she can give. Smile when she makes you happy, let her know when she makes you mad, and miss her when she's not there."
— Bob Marley

21
"You love me. Real or not real?"
I tell him, "Real."

— Suzanne Collins, Mockingjay

22

"Love looks not with the eyes, but with the mind,
And therefore is winged Cupid painted blind."
— William Shakespeare

23

"If you can make a woman laugh, you can make her do anything."
— Marilyn Monroe

24

"We're all a little weird. And life is a little weird. And when we find someone whose weirdness is compatible with ours, we join up with them and fall into mutually satisfying weirdness—and call it love—true love."

— Robert Fulghum, True Love

25

"Love is like the wind, you can't see it but you can feel it."
— Nicholas Sparks, A Walk to Remember

26

"People think a soul mate is your perfect fit, and that's what everyone wants. But a true soul mate is a mirror, the person who shows you everything that is holding you back, the person who brings you to your own attention so you can change your life.

A true soul mate is probably the most important person you'll ever meet, because they tear down your walls and smack you awake. But to live with a soul mate forever? Nah. Too painful. Soul mates, they come into your life just to reveal another layer of yourself to you, and then leave.

A soul mates purpose is to shake you up, tear apart your ego a little bit, show you your obstacles and addictions, break your heart open so new light can get in, make you so desperate and out of control that you have to transform your life, then introduce you to your spiritual master..."
— Elizabeth Gilbert, Eat, Pray, Love

27
"The real lover is the man who can thrill you by kissing your forehead or smiling into your eyes or just staring into space."
— Marilyn Monroe

28
"You don't love someone because they're perfect, you love them in spite of the fact that they're not."
— Jodi Picoult, My Sister's Keeper

29
"Love never dies a natural death. It dies because we don't know how to replenish its source. It dies of blindness and errors and betrayals. It dies of illness and wounds; it dies of weariness, of witherings, of tarnishings."
— Anaïs Nin

30
"There is nothing I would not do for those who are really my friends. I have no notion of loving people by halves, it is not my nature."

— Jane Austen, Northanger Abbey

31
"If I had a flower for every time I thought of you...I could walk through my garden forever."
— Alfred Tennyson

32
"So it's not gonna be easy. It's going to be really hard; we're gonna have to work at this everyday, but I want to do that because I want you. I want all of you, forever, everyday. You and me... everyday."
— Nicholas Sparks, The Notebook

33
"Tis better to have loved and lost Than never to have loved at all."
— Alfred Tennyson, In Memoriam

34

"I've been making a list of the things they don't teach you at school. They don't teach you how to love somebody. They don't teach you how to be famous. They don't teach you how to be rich or how to be poor. They don't teach you how to walk away from someone you don't love any longer. They don't teach you how to know what's going on in someone else's mind. They don't teach you what to say to someone who's dying. They don't teach you anything worth knowing."
— Neil Gaiman, The Sandman, Vol. 9: The Kindly Ones

35

"To die would be an awfully big adventure."
— J.M. Barrie, Peter Pan

36

"To love at all is to be vulnerable. Love anything and your heart will be wrung and possibly broken. If you want to make sure of keeping it intact you must give it to no one, not even an animal. Wrap it carefully round with hobbies and little luxuries; avoid all entanglements. Lock it up safe in the casket or coffin of your selfishness. But in that casket, safe, dark, motionless, airless, it will change. It will not be broken; it will become unbreakable, impenetrable, irredeemable. To love is to be vulnerable."
— C.S. Lewis, The Four Loves

37

"Just when you think it can't get any worse, it can. And just when you think it can't get any better, it can."
— Nicholas Sparks, At First Sight

38
"A lady's imagination is very rapid; it jumps from admiration to love, from love to matrimony in a moment."
— Jane Austen, Pride and Prejudice

39
"When someone loves you, the way they say your name is different. You know that your name is safe in their mouth."
— Jess C. Scott, The Intern

40
"I'm in love with you," he said quietly.

"Augustus," I said.

"I am," he said. He was staring at me, and I could see the corners of his eyes crinkling. "I'm in love with you, and I'm not in the business of denying myself the simple pleasure of saying true things. I'm in love with you, and I know that love is just a shout into the void, and that oblivion is inevitable, and that we're all doomed and that there will come a day when all our labor has been returned to dust, and I know the sun will swallow the only earth we'll ever have, and I am in love with you."
— John Green, The Fault in Our Stars

41

"The one you love and the one who loves you are never, ever the same person."
— Chuck Palahniuk, Invisible Monsters

42

"Love is needing someone. Love is putting up with someone's bad qualities because they somehow complete you."
— Sarah Dessen, This Lullaby

43

"Dumbledore watched her fly away, and as her silvery glow faded he turned back to Snape, and his eyes were full of tears.
"After all this time?"
"Always," said Snape."
— J.K. Rowling, Harry Potter and the Deathly Hallows

44

"Love is patient, love is kind. It does not envy, it does not boast, it is not proud. It is not rude, it is not self-

seeking, it is not easily angered, it keeps no record of wrongs. Love does not delight in evil but rejoices with the truth. It always protects, always trusts, always hopes, always perseveres."
— Holy Bible

45

"He's not perfect. You aren't either, and the two of you will never be perfect. But if he can make you laugh at least once, causes you to think twice, and if he admits to being human and making mistakes, hold onto him and give him the most you can. He isn't going to quote poetry, he's not thinking about you every moment, but he will give you a part of him that he knows you could break. Don't hurt him, don't change him, and don't expect for more than he can

give. Don't analyze. Smile when he makes you happy, yell when he makes you mad, and miss him when he's not there. Love hard when there is love to be had. Because perfect guys don't exist, but there's always one guy that is perfect for you."
— Bob Marley

46
"You are, and always have been, my dream."
— Nicholas Sparks, The Notebook

47
"When I despair, I remember that all through history the way of truth and love have always won. There have been tyrants and murderers, and for a time, they can seem invincible, but in the end, they always fall. Think of it-- always."

— Mahatma Gandhi

48
"I love you as certain dark things are
to be loved,
in secret, between the shadow and
the soul."
— Pablo Neruda, 100 Love Sonnets

49
"Perhaps all the dragons in our lives
are princesses who are only waiting to
see us act, just once, with beauty and
courage. Perhaps everything that
frightens us is, in its deepest essence,
something helpless that wants our
love."
— Rainer Maria Rilke, Letters to a
Young Poet

50

"You are my best friend as well as my lover, and I do not know which side of you I enjoy the most. I treasure each side, just as I have treasured our life together."
— Nicholas Sparks, The Notebook

51
"We love the things we love for what they are."
— Robert Frost

52
"We fell in love, despite our differences, and once we did, something rare and beautiful was created. For me, love like that has only happened once, and that's why every minute we spent together has been seared in my memory. I'll never forget a single moment of it."
— Nicholas Sparks, The Notebook

53

"In vain have I struggled. It will not do. My feelings will not be repressed. You must allow me to tell you how ardently I admire and love you."
— Jane Austen, Pride And Prejudice

54

"Where there is love there is life."
— Mahatma Gandhi

55

"Nobody has ever measured, not even poets, how much the heart can hold."
— Zelda Fitzgerald

56

"One is loved because one is loved. No reason is needed for loving."
— Paulo Coelho, The Alchemist

57

"I no longer believed in the idea of soul mates, or love at first sight. But I was beginning to believe that a very few times in your life, if you were lucky, you might meet someone who was exactly right for you. Not because he was perfect, or because you were, but because your combined flaws were arranged in a way that allowed two separate beings to hinge together."
— Lisa Kleypas, Blue-Eyed Devil

58

"I carry your heart with me (I carry it in my heart)I am never without it
(anywhere
I go you go,my dear; and whatever is done by only me is your doing,my darling)

I fear no fate (for you are my fate,my
sweet)I want no world (for beautiful
you are my world,my true)
and it's you are whatever a moon has
always meant and whatever a sun will
always sing is you

here is the deepest secret nobody
knows
(here is the root of the root and the
bud of the bud and the sky of the sky
of a tree called life; which grows
higher than the soul can hope or mind
can hide)
and this is the wonder that's keeping
the stars apart

I carry your heart (I carry it in my
heart)"
— E.E. Cummings

59

"Once upon a time there was a boy who loved a girl, and her laughter was a question he wanted to spend his whole life answering."
— Nicole Krauss, The History of Love

60
"The best love is the kind that awakens the soul and makes us reach for more, that plants a fire in our hearts and brings peace to our minds. And that's what you've given me. That's what I'd hoped to give you forever"
— Nicholas Sparks

61
"There are two basic motivating forces: fear and love. When we are afraid, we pull back from life. When we are in love, we open to all that life has to offer with passion, excitement,

and acceptance. We need to learn to love ourselves first, in all our glory and our imperfections. If we cannot love ourselves, we cannot fully open to our ability to love others or our potential to create. Evolution and all hopes for a better world rest in the fearlessness and open-hearted vision of people who embrace life."
— John Lennon

62
"And so the lion fell in love with the lamb..." he murmured. I looked away, hiding my eyes as I thrilled to the word.
"What a stupid lamb," I sighed.
"What a sick, masochistic lion."
— Stephenie Meyer, Twilight

63

"So, I love you because the entire universe conspired to help me find you."
— Paulo Coelho, The Alchemist

64

"I heard what you said. I'm not the silly romantic you think. I don't want the heavens or the shooting stars. I don't want gemstones or gold. I have those things already. I want...a steady hand. A kind soul. I want to fall asleep, and wake, knowing my heart is safe. I want to love, and be loved."
— Shana Abe

65

"And now I'm looking at you," he said, "and you're asking me if I still want you, as if I could stop loving you. As if I would want to give up the thing that makes me stronger than anything else

ever has. I never dared give much of myself to anyone before – bits of myself to the Lightwoods, to Isabelle and Alec, but it took years to do it – but, Clary, since the first time I saw you, I have belonged to you completely. I still do. If you want me."
— Cassandra Clare, City of Glass

✳ 66
"No relationship is perfect, ever. There are always some ways you have to bend, to compromise, to give something up in order to gain something greater...The love we have for each other is bigger than these small differences. And that's the key. It's like a big pie chart, and the love in a relationship has to be the biggest piece. Love can make up for a lot."
— Sarah Dessen, This Lullaby

67

"I would die for you. But I won't live for you."
— Stephen Chbosky

68

"Promise me you'll always remember: You're braver than you believe, and stronger than you seem, and smarter than you think."
— A.A. Milne

69

"This is a good sign, having a broken heart. It means we have tried for something."
— Elizabeth Gilbert, Eat, Pray, Love

70

"Some women choose to follow men, and some women choose to follow their dreams. If you're wondering

which way to go, remember that your career will never wake up and tell you that it doesn't love you anymore."
— Lady Gaga

71
"Life will break you. Nobody can protect you from that, and living alone won't either, for solitude will also break you with its yearning. You have to love. You have to feel. It is the reason you are here on earth. You are here to risk your heart. You are here to be swallowed up. And when it happens that you are broken, or betrayed, or left, or hurt, or death brushes near, let yourself sit by an apple tree and listen to the apples falling all around you in heaps, wasting their sweetness. Tell yourself you tasted as many as you could."

— Louise Erdrich, The Painted Drum LP

72
"Some people don't understand the promises they're making when they make them," I said.

"Right, of course. But you keep the promise anyway. That's what love is. Love is keeping the promise anyway."
— John Green, The Fault in Our Stars

73
"I would always rather be happy than dignified."
— Charlotte Brontë, Jane Eyre

74
"When we love, we always strive to become better than we are. When we strive to become better than we are,

everything around us becomes better
too."
— Paulo Coelho, The Alchemist

75
"What's meant to be will always find a
way"
— Trisha Yearwood

76
"Two people in love, alone, isolated
from the world, that's beautiful."
— Milan Kundera

77
"Promise Yourself
To be so strong that nothing
can disturb your peace of mind.
To talk health, happiness, and
prosperity
to every person you meet.

To make all your friends feel
that there is something in them
To look at the sunny side of
everything
and make your optimism come true.

To think only the best, to work only
for the best,
and to expect only the best.
To be just as enthusiastic about the
success of others
as you are about your own.

To forget the mistakes of the past
and press on to the greater
achievements of the future.
To wear a cheerful countenance at all
times
and give every living creature you
meet a smile.

To give so much time to the
improvement of yourself
that you have no time to criticize
others.
To be too large for worry, too noble
for anger, too strong for fear,
and too happy to permit the presence
of trouble.

To think well of yourself and to
proclaim this fact to the world,
not in loud words but great deeds.
To live in faith that the whole world is
on your side
so long as you are true to the best
that is in you."
— Christian D. Larson, Your Forces
and How to Use Them

78
"Every heart sings a song, incomplete,
until another heart whispers back.

Those who wish to sing always find a song. At the touch of a lover, everyone becomes a poet."
— Plato

79
"A book without words is like love without a kiss; it's empty."
— Andrew Wolfe

80
"A guy and a girl can be just friends, but at one point or another, they will fall for each other...Maybe temporarily, maybe at the wrong time, maybe too late, or maybe forever"
— Dave Matthews Band

81
"This above all: to thine own self be true,

And it must follow, as the night the day,
Thou canst not then be false to any man."
— William Shakespeare, Hamlet

82

"Doubt thou the stars are fire;
Doubt that the sun doth move;
Doubt truth to be a liar;
But never doubt I love."
— William Shakespeare, Hamlet

83

"Any man who can drive safely while kissing a pretty girl is simply not giving the kiss the attention it deserves."
— Albert Einstein

84

"The only thing worse than a boy who hates you: a boy that loves you."

— Markus Zusak, The Book Thief

85

"They didn't agree on much. In fact, they didn't agree on anything. They fought all the time and challenged each other ever day. But despite their differences, they had one important thing in common. They were crazy about each other."
— Nicholas Sparks, The Notebook

86

"The heart was made to be broken."
— Oscar Wilde

87

"I have a history of making decisions very quickly about men. I have always fallen in love fast and without measuring risks. I have a tendency not only to see the best in everyone, but

to assume that everyone is emotionally capable of reaching his highest potential. I have fallen in love more times than I care to count with the highest potential of a man, rather than with the man himself, and I have hung on to the relationship for a long time (sometimes far too long) waiting for the man to ascend to his own greatness. Many times in romance I have been a victim of my own optimism."
— Elizabeth Gilbert, Eat, Pray, Love

88

"I think if I've learned anything about friendship, it's to hang in, stay connected, fight for them, and let them fight for you. Don't walk away, don't be distracted, don't be too busy or tired, don't take them for granted. Friends are part of the glue that holds

life and faith together. Powerful
stuff."
— Jon Katz

89
"Love is a fire. But whether it is going
to warm your hearth or burn down
your house, you can never tell."
— Joan Crawford

90
"The more I know of the world, the
more I am convinced that I shall never
see a man whom I can really love. I
require so much!"
— Jane Austen, Sense And Sensibility

91
"What I want is to be needed. What I
need is to be indispensable to
somebody. Who I need is somebody
that will eat up all my free time, my

ego, my attention. Somebody
addicted to me. A mutual addiction."
— Chuck Palahniuk, Choke

92
"My daddy said, that the first time you
fall in love, it changes you forever and
no matter how hard you try, that
feeling just never goes away."
— Nicholas Sparks, The Notebook

93
"You could have had anything else in
the world, and you asked for me."
She smiled up at him. Filthy as he was,
covered in blood and dirt, he was the
most beautiful thing she'd ever seen.
"But I don't want anything else in the
world."
— Cassandra Clare, City of Glass

94

"Never love anyone who treats you like you're ordinary."
— Oscar Wilde

95

"I think you still love me, but we can't escape the fact that I'm not enough for you. I knew this was going to happen. So I'm not blaming you for falling in love with another woman. I'm not angry, either. I should be, but I'm not. I just feel pain. A lot of pain. I thought I could imagine how much this would hurt, but I was wrong."
— Haruki Murakami, South of the Border, West of the Sun

96

"You are the answer to every prayer I've offered. You are a song, a dream, a whisper, and I don't know how I

could have lived without you for as long as I have."
— Nicholas Sparks, The Notebook

97
"I can feel Peeta press his forehead into my temple and he asks, 'So now that you've got me, what are you going to do with me?' I turn into him. 'Put you somewhere you can't get hurt."
— Suzanne Collins, The Hunger Games

98
"I love you more than there are stars in the sky and fish in the sea."
— Nicholas Sparks

99
"Love doesn't just sit there, like a stone, it has to be made, like bread; remade all the time, made new."

— Ursula K. Le Guin, The Lathe of Heaven

100

"If you like her, if she makes you happy, and if you feel like you know her---then don't let her go."
— Nicholas Sparks, Message in a Bottle

101

"Have you ever been in love? Horrible isn't it? It makes you so vulnerable. It opens your chest and it opens up your heart and it means that someone can get inside you and mess you up. You build up all these defenses, you build up a whole suit of armor, so that nothing can hurt you, then one stupid person, no different from any other stupid person, wanders into your stupid life...You give them a piece of

you. They didn't ask for it. They did something dumb one day, like kiss you or smile at you, and then your life isn't your own anymore. Love takes hostages. It gets inside you. It eats you out and leaves you crying in the darkness, so simple a phrase like 'maybe we should be just friends' turns into a glass splinter working its way into your heart. It hurts. Not just in the imagination. Not just in the mind. It's a soul-hurt, a real gets-inside-you-and-rips-you-apart pain. I hate love."
— Neil Gaiman, The Sandman, Vol. 9: The Kindly Ones

102
"If all else perished, and he remained, I should still continue to be; and if all else remained, and he were

annihilated, the universe would turn to a mighty stranger."
— Emily Brontë, Wuthering Heights

103

"What I need is the dandelion in the spring. The bright yellow that means rebirth instead of destruction. The promise that life can go on, no matter how bad our losses. That it can be good again."
— Suzanne Collins, Mockingjay

104

"Love does not begin and end the way we seem to think it does. Love is a battle, love is a war; love is a growing up."
— James Baldwin

105

"There is always some madness in love. But there is also always some reason in madness."
— Friedrich Nietzsche

106
"We loved with a love that was more than love."
— Edgar Allan Poe

107
"The very essence of romance is uncertainty."
— Oscar Wilde, The Importance of Being Earnest and Other Plays

108
"The world is indeed full of peril and in it there are many dark places. But still there is much that is fair. And though in all lands, love is now

mingled with grief, it still grows, perhaps, the greater."
— J.R.R. Tolkien, The Lord of the Rings

109

"It hurts to let go. Sometimes it seems the harder you try to hold on to something or someone the more it wants to get away. You feel like some kind of criminal for having felt, for having wanted. For having wanted to be wanted. It confuses you, because you think that your feelings were wrong and it makes you feel so small because it's so hard to keep it inside when you let it out and it doesn't coma back. You're left so alone that you can't explain. Damn, there's nothing like that, is there? I've been there and you have too. You're nodding your head."

— Henry Rollins, The Portable Henry Rollins

110

"How many slams in an old screen door? Depends how loud you shut it. How many slices in a bread? Depends how thin you cut it. How much good inside a day? Depends how good you live 'em. How much love inside a friend? Depends how much you give 'em."
— Shel Silverstein

111

"And now these three remain: faith, hope and love. But the greatest of these is love."
— Holy Bible: King James Version

112

"Man may have discovered fire, but women discovered how to play with it."
— Candace Bushnell, Sex and the City

113
"Do you think I'm pretty?
I think you're beautiful
Beautiful?
You are so beautiful, it hurts sometimes."
— Richelle Mead, Vampire Academy

114
"He's more myself than I am. Whatever our souls are made of, his and mine are the same."
— Emily Brontë, Wuthering Heights

115
"Love is an irresistible desire to be irresistibly desired."

— Robert Frost

116
"Above all, don't lie to yourself. The man who lies to himself and listens to his own lie comes to a point that he cannot distinguish the truth within him, or around him, and so loses all respect for himself and for others. And having no respect he ceases to love."
— Fyodor Dostoyevsky, The Brothers Karamazov

117
"I love you like a fat kid loves cake!"
— Scott Adams

118
"And, in the end
The love you take
is equal to the love you make."

— Paul McCartney, The Beatles
Illustrated Lyrics

119
"I am not sure exactly what heaven
will be like, but I know that when we
die and it comes time for God to judge
us, he will not ask, 'How many good
things have you done in your life?'
rather he will ask, 'How much love did
you put into what you did?"
— Mother Teresa

120
"True love is rare, and it's the only
thing that gives life real meaning."
— Nicholas Sparks, Message in a
Bottle

121

"You know, when it works, love is pretty amazing. It's not overrated. There's a reason for all those songs."
— Sarah Dessen, This Lullaby

122
"Out beyond ideas of wrongdoing and rightdoing there is a field.
I'll meet you there.
When the soul lies down in that grass the world is too full to talk about."
— Rumi

123
"I love you. Remember. They cannot take it"
— Lauren Oliver, Delirium

124
"Sometimes it's a form of love just to talk to somebody that you have

nothing in common with and still be fascinated by their presence."
— David Byrne

125
"When love is not madness it is not love."
— Pedro Calderón de la Barca

126
"Gravitation is not responsible for people falling in love."
— Albert Einstein

127
"For the two of us, home isn't a place. It is a person. And we are finally home."
— Stephanie Perkins, Anna and the French Kiss

128

"To me, Fearless is not the absense of fear. It's not being completely unafraid. To me, Fearless is having fears. Fearless is having doubts. Lots of them. To me, Fearless is living in spite of those things that scare you to death."
— Taylor Swift

129
"One love, one heart, one destiny."
— Bob Marley

130
"Be careful of love. It'll twist your brain around and leave you thinking up is down and right is wrong."
— Rick Riordan, The Battle of the Labyrinth

 131

"We're all seeking that special person who is right for us. But if you've been through enough relationships, you begin to suspect there's no right person, just different flavors of wrong. Why is this? Because you yourself are wrong in some way, and you seek out partners who are wrong in some complementary way. But it takes a lot of living to grow fully into your own wrongness. And it isn't until you finally run up against your deepest demons, your unsolvable problems—the ones that make you truly who you are— that we're ready to find a lifelong mate. Only then do you finally know what you're looking for. You're looking for the wrong person. But not just any wrong person: the right wrong person—someone you lovingly gaze upon and think, "This is the problem I want to have."

I will find that special person who is
wrong for me in just the right way.

Let our scars fall in love."
— Galway Kinnell

132
"It was love at first sight, at last sight,
at ever and ever sight."
— Vladimir Nabokov, Lolita

133
"Of all forms of caution, caution in
love is perhaps the most fatal to true
happiness."
— Bertrand Russell, The Conquest of
Happiness

134
"If pain must come, may it come
quickly. Because I have a life to live,

and I need to live it in the best way possible. If he has to make a choice, may he make it now. Then I will either wait for him or forget him."
— Paulo Coelho, By the River Piedra I Sat Down and Wept

135
"Hate the sin, love the sinner."
— Mahatma Gandhi

136
"If you gave someone your heart and they died, did they take it with them? Did you spend the rest of forever with a hole inside you that couldn't be filled?"
— Jodi Picoult, Nineteen Minutes

137
"I have something I need to tell you," he says. I run my fingers along the

tendons in his hands and look back at him. "I might be in love with you." He smiles a little. "I'm waiting until I'm sure to tell you, though."
"That's sensible of you," I say, smiling too. "We should find some paper so you can make a list or a chart or something."
I feel his laughter against my side, his nose sliding along my jaw, his lips pressing my ear.
"Maybe I'm already sure," he says, "and I just don't want to frighten you." I laugh a little. "Then you should know better."
"Fine," he says. "Then I love you."
— Veronica Roth, Divergent

138
"Well, it seems to me that the best relationships - the ones that last - are frequently the ones that are rooted in

friendship. You know, one day you look at the person and you see something more than you did the night before. Like a switch has been flicked somewhere. And the person who was just a friend is... suddenly the only person you can ever imagine yourself with."
— Gillian Anderson

139
"Welcome to the wonderful world of jealousy, he thought. For the price of admission, you get a splitting headache, a nearly irresistable urge to commit murder, and an inferiority complex. Yippee."
— J.R. Ward, Dark Lover

140
"I was smiling yesterday,I am smiling today and I will smile tomorrow.

Simply because life is too short to cry
for anything."
— Santosh Kalwar, Quote Me
Everyday

141
"I do not trust people who don't love
themselves and yet tell me, 'I love
you.' There is an African saying which
is: Be careful when a naked person
offers you a shirt."
— Maya Angelou

142
"What Is Love? I have met in the
streets a very poor young man who
was in love. His hat was old, his coat
worn, the water passed through his
shoes and the stars through his soul"
— Victor Hugo

143

"Love is an untamed force. When we try to control it, it destroys us. When we try to imprison it, it enslaves us. When we try to understand it, it leaves us feeling lost and confused."
— Paulo Coelho

144
"You can't measure the mutual affection of two human beings by the number of words they exchange."
— Milan Kundera

145
"They say when you are missing someone that they are probably feeling the same, but I don't think it's possible for you to miss me as much as I'm missing you right now"
— Edna St. Vincent Millay

146

"If loving someone is putting them in a straitjacket and kicking them down a flight of stairs, then yes, I have loved a few people."
— Jarod Kintz, It Occurred to Me

147
"Love is so short, forgetting is so long."
— Pablo Neruda, Love: Ten Poems

148
"One day you will kiss a man you can't breathe without, and find that breath is of little consequence."
— Karen Marie Moning, Bloodfever

149
"If conversation was the lyrics, laughter was the music, making time spent together a melody that could be

replayed over and over without
getting stale."
— Nicholas Sparks

150
"Sorrow is how we learn to love. Your
heart isn't breaking. It hurts because
it's getting larger. The larger it gets,
the more love it holds."
— Rita Mae Brown, Riding Shotgun

151
"I think... if it is true that
there are as many minds as there
are heads, then there are as many
kinds of love as there are hearts."
— Leo Tolstoy, Anna Karenina

152
"I cannot fix on the hour, or the spot,
or the look or the words, which laid
the foundation. It is too long ago. I

was in the middle before I knew that I had begun."
— Jane Austen, Pride and Prejudice

✳ 153

"Let there be spaces in your togetherness, And let the winds of the heavens dance between you. Love one another but make not a bond of love: Let it rather be a moving sea between the shores of your souls. Fill each other's cup but drink not from one cup. Give one another of your bread but eat not from the same loaf. Sing and dance together and be joyous, but let each one of you be alone, Even as the strings of a lute are alone though they quiver with the same music. Give your hearts, but not into each other's keeping. For only the hand of Life can contain your hearts. And stand together, yet not too near

together: For the pillars of the temple stand apart, And the oak tree and the cypress grow not in each other's shadow."
— Kahlil Gibran, The Prophet

154

"The saddest people I've ever met in life are the ones who don't care deeply about anything at all. Passion and satisfaction go hand in hand, and without them, any happiness is only temporary, because there's nothing to make it last."
— Nicholas Sparks, Dear John

155

"I fell in love with her when we were together, then fell deeper in love with her in the years we were apart."
— Nicholas Sparks, Dear John

156

"If you love somebody, let them go, for if they return, they were always yours. If they don't, they never were."
— Kahlil Gibran

157

"Lost love is still love. It takes a different form, that's all. You can't see their smile or bring them food or tousle their hair or move them around a dance floor. But when those senses weaken another heightens. Memory. Memory becomes your partner. You nurture it. You hold it. You dance with it."
— Mitch Albom

158

"Sometimes love means letting go when you want to hold on tighter."
— Melissa Marr, Ink Exchange

159

"I crave your mouth, your voice, your
hair.
Silent and starving, I prowl through
the streets.
Bread does not nourish me, dawn
disrupts me, all day
I hunt for the liquid measure of your
steps.

I hunger for your sleek laugh,
your hands the color of a savage
harvest,
hunger for the pale stones of your
fingernails,
I want to eat your skin like a whole
almond.

I want to eat the sunbeam flaring in
your lovely body,

the sovereign nose of your arrogant
face,
I want to eat the fleeting shade of
your lashes,

and I pace around hungry, sniffing the
twilight,
hunting for you, for your hot heart,
Like a puma in the barrens of
Quitratue."
— Pablo Neruda

160
"What is hell? I maintain that it is the
suffering of being unable to love."
— Fyodor Dostoyevsky, The Brothers
Karamazov

161
"If you remember me, then I don't
care if everyone else forgets."

— Haruki Murakami, Kafka on the Shore

162

"Letting go doesn't mean that you don't care about someone anymore. It's just realizing that the only person you really have control over is yourself."
— Deborah Reber, Chicken Soup for the Teenage Soul: 101 Stories of Life, Love and Learning

163

"It's probably not just by chance that I'm alone. It would be very hard for a man to live with me, unless he's terribly strong. And if he's stronger than I, I'm the one who can't live with him. ... I'm neither smart nor stupid, but I don't think I'm a run-of-the-mill person. I've been in business without

being a businesswoman, I've loved without being a woman made only for love. The two men I've loved, I think, will remember me, on earth or in heaven, because men always remember a woman who caused them concern and uneasiness. I've done my best, in regard to people and to life, without precepts, but with a taste for justice."
— Coco Chanel

164
"Was it hard?" I ask.
Letting go?"
Not as hard as holding on to something that wasn't real."
— Lisa Schroeder

165
"I'm on Aslan's side even if there isn't any Aslan to lead it. I'm going to live

as like a Narnian as I can even if there
isn't any Narnia."
— C.S. Lewis, The Silver Chair

166

"How do I love thee? Let me count the
ways.
I love thee to the depth and breadth
and height
My soul can reach"
— Elizabeth Barrett Browning

167

"Peeta, how come I never know when
you're having a nightmare?" I say.
"I don't know. I don't think I cry out or
thrash around or anything. I just come
to, paralyzed with terror," he says.
"You should wake me," I say, thinking
about how I can interrupt his sleep
two or three times on a bad night.

About how long it can take to calm me down.
"It's not necessary. My nightmares are usually about losing you," he says.
"I'm okay once I realize you're here."
— Suzanne Collins, Catching Fire

168
"How do you spell 'love'?" - Piglet
"You don't spell it...you feel it." - Pooh"
— A.A. Milne

169
"Life, he realized, was much like a song. In the beginning there is mystery, in the end there is confirmation, but it's in the middle where all the emotion resides to make the whole thing worthwhile."
— Nicholas Sparks, The Last Song

170
"It is a curious thought, but it is only when you see people looking ridiculous that you realize just how much you love them. "
— Agatha Christie, An Autobiography

171
"We waste time looking for the perfect lover, instead of creating the perfect love."
— Tom Robbins

172
"It isn't possible to love and part. You will wish that it was. You can transmute love, ignore it, muddle it, but you can never pull it out of you. I know by experience that the poets are right: love is eternal."
— E.M. Forster, A Room with a View

173

"Before you, Bella, my life was like a moonless night. Very dark, but there were stars, points of light and reason. ...And then you shot across my sky like a meteor. Suddenly everything was on fire; there was brilliancy, there was beauty. When you were gone, when the meteor had fallen over the horizon, everything went black. Nothing had changed, but my eyes were blinded by the light. I couldn't see the stars anymore. And there was no more reason, for anything."
— Stephenie Meyer, New Moon

174

"And then he gives me a smile that just seems so genuinely sweet with just the right touch of shyness that unexpected warmth rushes through me."

— Suzanne Collins, The Hunger Games

175 ✳

"I read once that the ancient Egyptians had fifty words for sand & the Eskimos had a hundred words for snow. I wish I had a thousand words for love, but all that comes to mind is the way you move against me while you sleep & there are no words for that."
— Brian Andreas, Story People

176
"The man of knowledge must be able not only to love his enemies but also to hate his friends."
— Friedrich Nietzsche

177
"The heart has its reasons which reason knows not."

— Blaise Pascal

178
"Love can change a person the way a parent can change a baby- awkwardly, and often with a great deal of mess."
— Lemony Snicket, Horseradish: Bitter Truths You Can't Avoid

179
"Without you in my arms, I feel an emptiness in my soul. I find myself searching the crowds for your face - I know it's an impossibility, but I cannot help myself."
— Nicholas Sparks, Message in a Bottle

180
"The reason it hurts so much to separate is because our souls are connected. Maybe they always have

been and will be. Maybe we've lived a thousand lives before this one and in each of them we've found each other. And maybe each time, we've been forced apart for the same reasons. That means that this goodbye is both a goodbye for the past ten thousand years and a prelude to what will come."
— Nicholas Sparks, The Notebook

181

"If someone were to harm my family or a friend or somebody I love, I would eat them. I might end up in jail for 500 years, but I would eat them."
— Johnny Depp

182

"If she's amazing, she won't be easy. If she's easy, she won't be amazing. If she's worth it, you wont give up. If you

give up, you're not worthy. ... Truth is, everybody is going to hurt you; you just gotta find the ones worth suffering for."
— Bob Marley, Bob Marley - Guitar Chord Songbook

183
"The emotion that can break your heart is sometimes the very one that heals it..."
— Nicholas Sparks, At First Sight

184
"We have to allow ourselves to be loved by the people who really love us, the people who really matter. Too much of the time, we are blinded by our own pursuits of people to love us, people that don't even matter, while all that time we waste and the people who do love us have to stand on the

sidewalk and watch us beg in the streets! It's time to put an end to this. It's time for us to let ourselves be loved."
— C. JoyBell C.

185
"The beginning of love is the will to let those we love be perfectly themselves, the resolution not to twist them to fit our own image. If in loving them we do not love what they are, but only their potential likeness to ourselves, then we do not love them: we only love the reflection of ourselves we find in them"
— Thomas Merton, No Man Is an Island

186

"When you trip over love, it is easy to get up. But when you fall in love, it is impossible to stand again."
— Albert Einstein

187
"Then I realize what it is. It's him. Something about him makes me feel like I am about to fall. Or turn to liquid. Or burst into flames."
— Veronica Roth, Divergent

188
"When someone is in your heart, they're never truly gone. They can come back to you, even at unlikely times."
— Mitch Albom, For One More Day

189
"Don't cry over someone who wouldn't cry over you."

— Lauren Conrad

190

"You know it's never fifty-fifty in a marriage. It's always seventy-thirty, or sixty-forty. Someone falls in love first. Someone puts someone else up on a pedestal. Someone works very hard to keep things rolling smoothly; someone else sails along for the ride."
— Jodi Picoult, Mercy

191

"The bond forged between us was not one that could be broken by absence, distance, or time. And no matter how much more special or beautiful or brilliant or perfect than me he might be, he was as irreversibly altered as I was. As I would always belong to him, so would he always be mine."
— Stephenie Meyer, New Moon

192

"to love life, to love it even
when you have no stomach for it
and everything you've held dear
crumbles like burnt paper in your
hands,
your throat filled with the silt of it.
When grief sits with you, its tropical
heat
thickening the air, heavy as water
more fit for gills than lungs;
when grief weights you like your own
flesh
only more of it, an obesity of grief,
you think, How can a body withstand
this?
Then you hold life like a face
between your palms, a plain face,
no charming smile, no violet eyes,
and you say, yes, I will take you
I will love you, again."

— Ellen Bass

193
"Every one of us is, in the cosmic perspective, precious. If a human disagrees with you, let him live. In a hundred billion galaxies, you will not find another."
— Carl Sagan, Cosmos

194
"I will love you always. When this red hair is white, I will still love you. When the smooth softness of youth is replaced by the delicate softness of age, I will still want to touch your skin. When your face is full of the lines of every smile you have ever smiled, of every surprise I have seen flash through your eyes, when every tear you have ever cried has left its mark upon your face,I will treasure you all

the more, because I was there to see
it all. I will share your life with you,
Meredith, and I will love you until the
last breath leaves your body or mine."
— Laurell K. Hamilton, A Lick of Frost

195
"A purpose of human life, no matter
who is controlling it, is to love
whoever is around to be loved."
— Kurt Vonnegut, The Sirens of Titan

196
"I'm not sentimental--I'm as romantic
as you are. The idea, you know,
is that the sentimental person thinks
things will last--the romantic
person has a desperate confidence
that they won't."
— F. Scott Fitzgerald, This Side of
Paradise

197

"When I am with you, we stay up all night.
When you're not here, I can't go to sleep.
Praise God for those two insomnias!
And the difference between them."
— Rumi

198

"Maybe...you'll fall in love with me all over again."
"Hell," I said, "I love you enough now. What do you want to do? Ruin me?"
"Yes. I want to ruin you."
"Good," I said. "That's what I want too."
— Ernest Hemingway, A Farewell to Arms

199

"Watch out for intellect,

because it knows so much it knows
nothing
and leaves you hanging upside down,
mouthing knowledge as your heart
falls out of your mouth."
— Anne Sexton, The Complete Poems

200
"If there is no love in the world, we
will make a new world, and we will
give it walls, and we will furnish it with
soft, red interiors, from the inside out,
and give it a knocker that resonates
like a diamond falling to a jeweller's
felt so that we should never hear it.
Love me, because love doesn't exist,
and I have tried everything that does."
— Jonathan Safran Foer, Everything Is
Illuminated

201

"Romance is the glamour which turns the dust of everyday life into a golden haze. "
— Elinor Glyn

202
"I wasn't actually in love, but I felt a sort of tender curiosity."
— F. Scott Fitzgerald, The Great Gatsby

203
"Sometimes when I look at you, I feel I'm gazing at a distant star.
It's dazzling, but the light is from tens of thousands of years ago.
Maybe the star doesn't even exist any more. Yet sometimes that light seems more real to me than anything."
— Haruki Murakami, South of the Border, West of the Sun

204

"You'll get over it..." It's the clichés that cause the trouble. To lose someone you love is to alter your life for ever. You don't get over it because 'it" is the person you loved. The pain stops, there are new people, but the gap never closes. How could it? The particularness of someone who mattered enough to grieve over is not made anodyne by death. This hole in my heart is in the shape of you and no-one else can fit it. Why would I want them to?"
— Jeanette Winterson, Written on the Body

205

"I could not tell you if I loved you the first moment I saw you, or if it was the second or third or fourth. But I remember the first moment I looked

at you walking toward me and realized that somehow the rest of the world seemed to vanish when I was with you."
— Cassandra Clare, Clockwork Prince

206
"About all you can do in life is be who you are. Some people will love you for you. Most will love you for what you can do for them, and some won't like you at all."
— Rita Mae Brown

207
"As if you were on fire from within. The moon lives in the lining of your skin."
— Pablo Neruda

208

"She leaned down and looked at his lifeless face and Leisel kissed her best friend, Rudy Steiner, soft and true on his lips. He tasted dusty and sweet. He tasted like regret in the shadows of trees and in the glow of the anarchist's suit collection. She kissed him long and soft, and when she pulled herself away, she touched his mouth with her fingers...She did not say goodbye. She was incapable, and after a few more minutes at his side, she was able to tear herself from the ground. It amazes me what humans can do, even when streams are flowing down their faces and they stagger on..."
— Markus Zusak, The Book Thief

209

"All I ever wanted was to reach out and touch another human being not

just with my hands but with my
heart."
— Tahereh Mafi, Shatter Me

210
"I have feelings too. I am still human.
All I want is to be loved, for myself
and for my talent. "
— Marilyn Monroe

211
"When I say it's you I like, I'm talking
about that part of you that knows that
life is far more than anything you can
ever see or hear or touch. That deep
part of you that allows you to stand
for those things without which
humankind cannot survive. Love that
conquers hate, peace that rises
triumphant over war, and justice that
proves more powerful than greed."
— Fred Rogers

212

"You yourself, as much as anybody in the entire universe, deserve your love and affection"
— Gautama Buddha

213

"The power of a glance has been so much abused in love stories, that it has come to be disbelieved in. Few people dare now to say that two beings have fallen in love because they have looked at each other. Yet it is in this way that love begins, and in this way only."
— Victor Hugo, Les Misérables

214

"I wonder how many people don't get the one they want, but end up with the one they're supposed to be with."

— Fannie Flagg, Fried Green Tomatoes
at the Whistle Stop Cafe

215
"The highest function of love is that it
makes the loved one a unique and
irreplaceable being."
— Tom Robbins, Jitterbug Perfume

216
"Love does not consist of gazing at
each other, but in looking outward
together in the same direction."
— Antoine de Saint-Exupéry, Airman's
Odyssey

217
"What's this?" he demanded, looking
from Clary to his companions, as if
they might know what she was doing
there.

"It's a girl," Jace said, recovering his composure. "Surely you've seen girls before, Alec. Your sister Isabelle is one."
— Cassandra Clare, City of Bones

218

"Love is not affectionate feeling, but a steady wish for the loved person's ultimate good as far as it can be obtained."
— C.S. Lewis

219

"In time, the hurt began to fade and it was easier to just let it go. At least I thought it was. But in every boy I met in the next few years, I found myself looking for you, and when the feelings got too strong, I'd write you another letter. But I never sent them for fear of what I might find. By then, you'd

gone on with your life and I didn't
want to think about you loving
someone else. I wanted to remember
us like we were that summer. I didn't
ever want to lose that."
— Nicholas Sparks, The Notebook

220
"Who, being loved, is poor?"
— Oscar Wilde

221
"One word
Frees us of all the weight and pain of
life:
That word is love."
— Sophocles

222
"The love of learning, the sequestered
nooks,
And all the sweet serenity of books"

— Henry Wadsworth Longfellow

223
"I sought to hear the voice of God and climbed the topmost steeple, but God declared: "Go down again - I dwell among the people."
— John Henry Newman

224
"My wish is that you may be loved to the point of madness."
— André Breton, What is Surrealism?: Selected Writings

225
"love, I've come to understand is more than three words mumbled before bedtime."
— Nicholas Sparks

226

"From childhood's hour I have not been. As others were, I have not seen. As others saw, I could not awaken. My heart to joy at the same tone. And all I loved, I loved alone."
— Edgar Allan Poe

227
"Things we lose have a way of coming back to us in the end, if not always in the way we expect."
— J.K. Rowling, Harry Potter and the Order of the Phoenix

228
"If you love and get hurt, love more. If you love more and hurt more, love even more.

If you love even more and get hurt even more, love some more until it hurts no more..."

— William Shakespeare

229
"Be with me always - take any form - drive me mad! only do not leave me in this abyss, where I cannot find you! Oh, God! it is unutterable! I can not live without my life! I can not live without my soul!"
— Emily Brontë, Wuthering Heights

230
"I won't ever leave you, even though you're always leaving me."
— Audrey Niffenegger, The Time Traveler's Wife

231
"Love has nothing to do with what you are expecting to get - only with what you are expecting to give - which is everything"

— Katharine Hepburn, Me: Stories of
My Life

232
"Respect was invented to cover the
empty place where love should be."
— Leo Tolstoy, Anna Karenina

233
"When we meet someone and fall in
love, we have a sense that the whole
universe is on our side. And yet if
something goes wrong, there is
nothing left! How is it possible for the
beauty that was there only minutes
before to vanish so quickly? Life
moves very fast. It rushes from
heaven to hell in a matter of seconds."
— Paulo Coelho, Eleven Minutes

234

"This is what we call love. When you are loved, you can do anything in creation. When you are loved, there's no need at all to understand what's happening, because everything happens within you."
— Paulo Coelho, The Alchemist

235
"Time was passing like a hand waving from a train I wanted to be on.
I hope you never have to think about anything as much as I think about you."
— Jonathan Safran Foer

236
"I want to be in a relationship where you telling me you love me is just a ceremonious validation of what you already show me."

— Steve Maraboli, Life, the Truth, and Being Free

237
"There is only one page left to write on. I will fill it with words of only one syllable. I love. I have loved. I will love."
— Audrey Niffenegger, The Time Traveler's Wife

238
"If we have no peace, it is because we have forgotten that we belong to each other."
— Mother Teresa

239*
"When God Created Mothers"
When the Good Lord was creating mothers, He was into His sixth day of "overtime" when the angel appeared

and said. "You're doing a lot of fiddling around on this one."

And God said, "Have you read the specs on this order?" She has to be completely washable, but not plastic. Have 180 moveable parts...all replaceable. Run on black coffee and leftovers. Have a lap that disappears when she stands up. A kiss that can cure anything from a broken leg to a disappointed love affair. And six pairs of hands."

The angel shook her head slowly and said. "Six pairs of hands.... no way."

It's not the hands that are causing me problems," God remarked, "it's the three pairs of eyes that mothers have to have."

That's on the standard model?" asked the angel. God nodded.

One pair that sees through closed doors when she asks, 'What are you kids doing in there?' when she already knows. Another here in the back of her head that sees what she shouldn't but what she has to know, and of course the ones here in front that can look at a child when he goofs up and say. 'I understand and I love you' without so much as uttering a word."

God," said the angel touching his sleeve gently, "Get some rest tomorrow...."

I can't," said God, "I'm so close to creating something so close to myself. Already I have one who heals herself when she is sick...can feed a family of six on one pound of hamburger...and can get a nine year old to stand under a shower."

The angel circled the model of a mother very slowly. "It's too soft," she sighed.

But tough!" said God excitedly. "You can imagine what this mother can do or endure."

Can it think?"

Not only can it think, but it can reason and compromise," said the Creator.

Finally, the angel bent over and ran her finger across the cheek.

There's a leak," she pronounced. "I told You that You were trying to put too much into this model."

It's not a leak," said the Lord, "It's a tear."

What's it for?"

It's for joy, sadness, disappointment, pain, loneliness, and pride."

You are a genius, " said the angel.

Somberly, God said, "I didn't put it there."
— Erma Bombeck, When God Created Mothers

240
"But love is always new. Regardless of whether we love once, twice, or a

dozen times in our life, we always face a brand-new situation. Love can consign us to hell or to paradise, but it always takes us somewhere. We simply have to accept it, because it is what nourishes our existence. If we reject it, we die of hunger, because we lack the courage to stretch out a hand and pluck the fruit from the branches of the tree of life. We have to take love where we find it, even if that means hours, days, weeks of disappointment and sadness.

The moment we begin to seek love, love begins to seek us. And to save us."
— Paulo Coelho, By the River Piedra

241

"You are the one girl that made me risk eveything for a future worth having."
— Simone Elkeles, Perfect Chemistry

242
"Someday you'll find someone special again. People who've been in love once usually do. It's in their nature."
— Nicholas Sparks, Message in a Bottle

243
"Romance is thinking about your significant other, when you are supposed to be thinking about something else."
— Nicholas Sparks

244
"I'm about to make a wild, extreme and severe relationship rule: the word

busy is a load of crap and is most often used by assholes. The word "busy" is the relationship Weapon of Mass Destruction. It seems like a good excuse, but in fact in every silo you uncover, all you're going to find is a man who didn't care enough to call. Remember men are never to busy to get what they want."
— Greg Behrendt

245
"Love is how you stay alive, even after you are gone."
— Mitch Albom

246
"It's not the face, but the expressions on it. It's not the voice, but what you say. It's not how you look in that body, but the thing you do with it. You are beautiful."

— Stephenie Meyer, The Host

247
"Promise me you'll never forget me because if I thought you would, I'd never leave."
— A.A. Milne

248
"Anyone who falls in love is searching for the missing pieces of themselves. So anyone who's in love gets sad when they think of their lover. It's like stepping back inside a room you have fond memories of, one you haven't seen in a long time."
— Haruki Murakami

249
"To love oneself is the beginning of a lifelong romance."
— Oscar Wilde, An Ideal Husband

250

"You know how they say you only hurt the ones you love? Well, it works both ways."
— Chuck Palahniuk, Fight Club

251

"If you love something set it free, but don't be surprised if it comes back with herpes."
— Chuck Palahniuk

252

"The human heart is a strange vessel. Love and hatred can exist side by side."
— Scott Westerfeld

253

"O Romeo, Romeo, wherefore art thou Romeo?

Deny thy father refuse thy name, thou art thyself thou not a montegue, what is montegue? tis nor hand nor foot nor any other part belonging to a man What is in a name?
That which we call a rose by any other name would smell as sweet,
So Romeo would were he not Romeo called retain such dear perfection to which he owes without that title, Romeo, Doth thy name!
And for that name which is no part of thee, take all thyself."
— William Shakespeare

254
"True love is not so much a matter of romance as it is a matter of anxious concern for the well-being of one's companion."

— Gordon B. Hinckley, Stand a Little Taller: Counsel and Inspiration for Each Day of the Year

255

"Tears shed for another person are not a sign of weakness. They are a sign of a pure heart."
— José N. Harris, MI VIDA: A Story of Faith, Hope and Love

256

"I've been fighting to be who I am all my life. What's the point of being who I am, if I can't have the person who was worth all the fighting for?"
— Stephanie Lennox, I Don't Remember You

257

"Find what you love and let it kill you."
— Charles Bukowski

258

"Why are old lovers able to become friends? Two reasons. They never truly loved each other, or they love each other still."
— Whitney Otto, How to Make an American Quilt

259

"My name is Ashallyn'darkmyr Tallyn, third son of the Unseelie Court...Let it be known--from this day forth, I vow to protect Meghan Chase, daughter of the Summer King, with my sword, my honor, and my life. Her desires are mine. Her wishes are mine. Should even the world stand against her, my blade will be at her side. And should it fail to protect her, let my own existence be forfeit. This I swear, on my honor, my True Name, and my life.

From this day on..." His voice went even softer, but I still heard it as though he whispered it into my ear. "I am yours."
— Julie Kagawa, The Iron Queen

260
"If a thing loves, it is infinite."
— William Blake

261
"Love is a decision, it is a judgment, it is a promise. If love were only a feeling, there would be no basis for the promise to love each other forever. A feeling comes and it may go. How can I judge that it will stay forever, when my act does not involve judgment and decision."
— Erich Fromm, The Art of Loving

262

"In your light I learn how to love. In your beauty, how to make poems. You dance inside my chest where no-one sees you, but sometimes I do, and that sight becomes this art."
— Rumi

263
"Come sleep with me: We won't make Love,Love will make us."
— Julio Cortázar

264
"The world was collapsing, and the only thing that really mattered to me was that she was alive."
— Rick Riordan, The Last Olympian

265
"and he suddenly knew that if she killed herself, he would die. Maybe not immediately, maybe not with the

same blinding rush of pain, but it would happen. You couldn't live for very long without a heart."
— Jodi Picoult

266
"I told you. You don't love someone because of their looks or their clothes or their car. You love them because they sing a song only your heart can understand."
— L.J. Smith

267
"Yes, I was infatuated with you: I am still. No one has ever heightened such a keen capacity of physical sensation in me. I cut you out because I couldn't stand being a passing fancy. Before I give my body, I must give my thoughts, my mind, my dreams. And you weren't having any of those."

— Sylvia Plath, The Unabridged
Journals of Sylvia Plath

268
"The great tragedy of life is not that
men perish, but that they cease to
love."
— W. Somerset Maugham

269
"Let me not to the marriage of true
minds
Admit impediments. Love is not love
Which alters when it alteration finds,
Or bends with the remover to remove.
O no, it is an ever-fixed mark
That looks on tempests and is never
shaken;
It is the star to every wand'ring
barque,
Whose worth's unknown, although his
height be taken.

Love's not Time's fool, though rosy lips and cheeks
Within his bending sickle's compass come;
Love alters not with his brief hours and weeks,
But bears it out even to the edge of doom.
If this be error and upon me proved,
I never writ, nor no man ever loved."
— William Shakespeare, Great Sonnets

270
"You are like nobody since I love you."
— Pablo Neruda

271
"Love sucks. Sometimes it feels good. Sometimes it's just another way to bleed."
— Laurell K. Hamilton, Blue Moon

272

"I know that's what people say-- you'll get over it. I'd say it, too. But I know it's not true. Oh, youll be happy again, never fear. But you won't forget. Every time you fall in love it will be because something in the man reminds you of him."
— Betty Smith, A Tree Grows in Brooklyn

273

"It is good to love many things, for therein lies the true strength, and whosoever loves much performs much, and can accomplish much, and what is done in love is well done."
— Vincent van Gogh

274

"I like flaws. I think they make things interesting."
— Sarah Dessen, The Truth About Forever

275
"Friendship marks a life even more deeply than love. Love risks degenerating into obsession, friendship is never anything but sharing."
— Elie Wiesel

276
"To lose balance sometimes for love is part of living a balanced life."
— Elizabeth Gilbert, Eat, Pray, Love

277
"Love is . . . Being happy for the other person when they are happy, Being

sad for the person when they are sad,
Being together in good times, And
being together in bad times.
LOVE IS THE SOURCE OF STRENGTH.

Love is . . . Being honest with yourself
at all times, Being honest with the
other person at all times, Telling,
listening, respecting the truth, And
never pretending.
LOVE IS THE SOURCE OF REALITY.

Love is . . . An understanding so
complete that you feel as if you are a
part of the other person, Accepting
the other person just the way they
are, And not trying to change them to
be something else.
LOVE IS THE SOURCE OF UNITY.

Love is . . . The freedom to pursue
your own desires while sharing your

experiences with the other person,
The growth of one individual
alongside of and together with the
growth of another individual.
LOVE IS THE SOURCE OF SUCCESS.

Love is . . . The excitement of planning
things together, The excitement of
doing things together.
LOVE IS THE SOURCE OF THE FUTURE.
Love is . . . The fury of the storm, The
calm in the rainbow.
LOVE IS THE SOURCE OF PASSION.

Love is . . . Giving and taking in a daily
situation, Being patient with each
other's needs and desires.
LOVE IS THE SOURCE OF SHARING.

Love is . . . Knowing that the other
person will always be with you
regardless of what happens, Missing

the other person when they are away
but remaining near in heart at all
times.
LOVE IS THE SOURCE OF SECURITY.
LOVE IS . . . THE SOURCE OF LIFE!"
— Susan Polis Schutz

278
"sometimes you don't need a goal in
life, you don't need to know the big
picture. you just need to know what
you're going to do next!"
— Sophie Kinsella, The Undomestic
Goddess

279
"Even more, I had never meant to love
him. One thing I truly knew - knew it
in the pit of my stomach, in the center
of my bones, knew it from the crown
of my head to the soles of my feet,
knew it deep in my empty chest - was

how love gave someone the power to break you"
— Stephenie Meyer, Twilight

280

"Just because you're beautiful and perfect, it's made you conceited."
— William Goldman, The Princess Bride

281

"Wherever you will go,
I will let you down,
But this lullaby goes on."
— Sarah Dessen, This Lullaby

282

"Yet each man kills the thing he loves
By each let this be heard
Some do it with a bitter look
Some with a flattering word
The coward does it with a kiss

The brave man with a sword"
— Oscar Wilde, The Ballad Of Reading
Gaol

283
"I'm oxygen and he's dying to
breathe."
— Tahereh Mafi, Shatter Me

284
"In real life, love has to be possible.
Even if it is not returned right away,
love can only survive when the hope
exists that you will be able to win over
the person you desire."
— Paulo Coelho, By the River Piedra I
Sat Down and Wept

285
"No matter how much you think you
love somebody, you'll step back when

the pool of their blood edges up too close."
— Chuck Palahniuk, Invisible Monsters

286
"When you love someone, you say their name different. Like it's safe inside your mouth."
— Jodi Picoult, Handle With Care

287
"One cannot think well, love well, sleep well, if one has not dined well."
— Virginia Woolf, A Room of One's Own

288
"You can search throughout the entire universe for someone who is more deserving of your love and affection than you are yourself, and that person is not to be found anywhere. You,

yourself, as much as anybody in the entire universe, deserve your love and affection."
— Gautama Buddha

289
"It doesn't matter who you are or what you look like, so long as somebody loves you."
— Roald Dahl, The Witches

290
"Poets often describe love as an emotion that we can't control, one that overwhelms logic and common sense. That's what it was like for me. I didn't plan on falling in love with you, and I doubt if you planned on falling in love with me. But once we met, it was clear that neither of us could control what was happening to us. We fell in love, despite our differences, and

once we did, something rare and beautiful was created. For me, love like that has happened only once, and that's why every minute we spent together has been seared in my memory. I'll never forget a single moment of it."
— Nicholas Sparks, The Notebook

291
"If a girl starts out all casual with a guy and she doesn't tell him that she wants a relationship, it will never become a relationship. If you give the guy the impression that casual is okay with you, that's all he'll ever want. Be straight with him from the start. If he gets scared and runs away, he wasn't right for you."
— Susane Colasanti, Waiting For You

292

"The course of true love never did run smooth."
— William Shakespeare,

293
"People have forgotten this truth," the fox said. "But you mustn't forget it. You become responsible forever for what you've tamed. You're responsible for your rose."
— Antoine de Saint-Exupéry, The Little Prince

294
"Sometimes when I'm alone, I take the pearl from where it lives in my pocket and try to remember the boy with the bread, the strong arms that warded off nightmares on the train, the kisses in the arena."
— Suzanne Collins, Mockingjay

295

"It is possible to be in love with you just because of who you are."
— Maggie Stiefvater, Shiver

296

"I, um, I have this problem. I broke up with my boyfriend, you see. And I'm pretty upset about it, so I wanted to talk to my best friend. [...] The thing is, they're both you."
— Jodi Picoult, The Pact

297

"I'm lonely. Why do you think I had to learn to act so independent? I also get mad too quickly, and I hog the covers, and my second toe is longer than my big one. My hair has it's own zip code. Plus, I get certifiably crazy when I've got PMS. You don't love someone because they're perfect. You love

them in spite of the fact that they're
not."
— Jodi Picoult, My Sister's Keeper

298
"Love, n. A temporary insanity curable
by marriage."
— Ambrose Bierce, The Unabridged
Devil's Dictionary

299
"Love is a better master than duty."
— Albert Einstein

300
"I like not only to be loved, but also to
be told that I am loved. I am not sure
that you are of the same mind. But
the realm of silence is large enough
beyond the grave. This is the world of
light and speech, and I shall take leave
to tell you that you are very dear."

— George Eliot

301
"Eleanor was right. She never looked nice. She looked like art, and art wasn't supposed to look nice; it was supposed to make you feel something."
— Rainbow Rowell, Eleanor & Park

302
"By the time you swear you're his,
Shivering and sighing.
And he vows his passion is,
Infinite, undying.
Lady make note of this --
One of you is lying."
— Dorothy Parker

303
"You have a... remarkable memory."

"I remember everything about you. You're the one who wasn't paying attention."
— Suzanne Collins, The Hunger Games

304
"Someone I loved once gave me a box full of darkness. It took me years to understand that this too, was a gift."
— Mary Oliver

305
"No woman wants to be in submission to a man who isn't in submission to God!"
— T.D. Jakes

306
"She wanted something else, something different, something more. Passion and romance, perhaps, or maybe quiet conversations in candlelit

rooms, or perhaps something as simple as not being second."
— Nicholas Sparks, The Notebook

307

"It's dark now and I am very tired. I love you, always. Time is nothing."
— Audrey Niffenegger, The Time Traveler's Wife

308

"That's what people do who love you. They put their arms around you and love you when you're not so lovable."
— Deb Caletti

309 ✳

"I was always hungry for love. Just once, I wanted to know what it was like to get my fill of it -- to be fed so much love I couldn't take any more. Just once. "

— Haruki Murakami, Norwegian Wood

310
"I want morning and noon and nightfall with you. I want your tears, your smiles, your kisses...the smell of your hair, the taste of your skin, the touch of your breath on my face. I want to see you in the final hour of my life...to lie in your arms as I take my last breath."
— Lisa Kleypas, Again the Magic

311
"To fear love is to fear life, and those who fear life are already 3-parts dead."
— Bertrand Russell

312

"You're in a car with a beautiful boy, and he won't tell you that he loves you, but he loves you. And you feel like you've done something terrible, like robbed a liquor store, or swallowed pills, or shoveled yourself a grave in the dirt, and you're tired. You're in a car with a beautiful boy, and you're trying not to tell him that you love him, and you're trying to choke down the feeling, and you're trembling, but he reaches over and he touches you, like a prayer for which no words exist, and you feel your heart taking root in your body, like you've discovered something you didn't even have a name for."
— Richard Siken

313
"The really important kind of freedom involves attention, and awareness,

and discipline, and effort, and being able truly to care about other people and to sacrifice for them, over and over, in myriad petty little unsexy ways, every day."
— David Foster Wallace, This Is Water

314

"I think it is all a matter of love; the more you love a memory the stronger and stranger it becomes"
— Vladimir Nabokov

315

"You're like a song that I heard when I was a little kid but forgot I knew until I heard it again."
— Maggie Stiefvater, Lament: The

316

"Moments, when lost, can't be found again. They're just gone."

— Jenny Han, The Summer I Turned Pretty

317

"Perhaps, after all, romance did not come into one's life with pomp and blare, like a gay knight riding down; perhaps it crept to one's side like an old friend through quiet ways; perhaps it revealed itself in seeming prose, until some sudden shaft of illumination flung athwart its pages betrayed the rhythm and the music, perhaps . . . perhaps . . . love unfolded naturally out of a beautiful friendship, as a golden-hearted rose slipping from its green sheath."
— L.M. Montgomery

318

"here she is, all mine, trying her best to give me all she can. How could I

ever hurt her? But I didn't understand then. That I could hurt somebody so badly she would never recover. That a person can, just by living, damage another human being beyond repair."
— Haruki Murakami, South of the

319
"Snape's patronus was a doe,' said Harry, 'the same as my mother's because he loved her for nearly all of his life, from when they were children."
— J.K. Rowling, Harry Potter and the Deathly Hallows

320
"When I saw you I fell in love, and you smiled because you knew."
— Arrigo Boito

321

"Being with you never felt wrong. It's the one thing I did right. You're the one thing I did right."
— Becca Fitzpatrick, Crescendo

322
"When I look in the mirror, I know I'm looking at someone who isn't sure she deserves to be loved at all."
— Nicholas Sparks, Dear John

323 X
You ARE
"She was my dream. She made me who I am, and holding her in my arms was more natural to me than my own heartbeat. I think about her all the time. Even now, when I'm sitting here, I think about her. There could never have been another." only you
— Nicholas Sparks, The Notebook

324

"I'd learned that some things are best kept secret."
— Nicholas Sparks, Dear John

325
"If you're a bird... I'm a bird..."
— Nicholas Sparks, The Notebook

326
"Sometimes God allows what he hates to accomplish what he loves."
— Joni Eareckson Tada, The God I Love

327
"Well?" Ron said finally, looking up at Harry. "How was it?"
Harry considered it for a moment.
"Wet," he said truthfully.
Ron made a noise that might have indicated jubilation or disgust, it was hard to tell.

"Because she was crying," Harry continued heavily.

"Oh," said Ron, his smile faded slightly. "Are you that bad at kissing?"

"Dunno," said Harry, who hadn't considered this, and immediately felt rather worried. "Maybe I am."
— J.K. Rowling, Harry Potter and the Order of the Phoenix

328

"I don't want to lose you.' His voice almost a whisper. Seeing his haggard expression, she took his hand and squeezed it, then reluctantly let it go. She could feel the tears again, and she fought them back. 'But you don't want to keep me, either, do you?' To that, he had no response."
— Nicholas Sparks, The Rescue

329

"He stared at her, knowing with certainty that he was falling in love. He pulled her close and kissed her beneath a blanket of stars, wondering how on earth he'd been lucky enough to find her."
— Nicholas Sparks, The Last Song

330
"The fate of your heart is your choice and no one else gets a vote"
— Sarah Dessen, This Lullaby

331
"You really love her don't you," she said.
With all my heart."
She looked as sad as I'd ever seen her.
What's your heart telling you to do?"
I don't know."
Maybe", she said gently,"You're trying to hard to hear it."

— Nicholas Sparks

332
"If you can capture a woman's imagination, then you will have her. But imagination is a strange creature. It needs time and distance to function properly."
— Kathleen Tessaro

333
"We're staying together," he promised. "You're not getting away from me. Never again."
— Rick Riordan, The Mark of Athena

334
"[H]iding how you really feel and trying to make everyone happy doesn't make you nice, it just makes you a liar."
— Jenny O'Connell, The Book of Luke

335

"Spending time with you showed me
what I've been missing in my life."
— Nicholas Sparks, The Choice

336

"I was blind and heart broken and
didn't want to do anything and Gus
burst into my room and shouted, "I
have wonderful news!" And I was like,
"I don't really want to hear wonderful
news right now," and Gus said, "This is
wonderful news you want to hear,"
and I asked him, "Fine, what is it?"
and he said, "You are going to live a
good and long life filled with great and
terrible moments that you cannot
even imagine yet!"
— John Green, The Fault in Our Stars

 337

"I've been in love before, it's like a narcotic. At first it brings the euphoria of complete surrender. The next day you want more. You're not addicted yet, but you like the sensation, and you think you can still control things. You think about the person you love for two minutes then forget them for three hours. But then you get used to that person, and you begin to be completely dependent on them. Now you think about him for three hours and forget him for two minutes. If he's not there, you feel like an addict who can't get a fix. And just as addicts steal and humiliate themselves to get what they need, you're willing to do anything for love."- By the River Piedra I Sat Down and Wept"
— Paulo Coelho

338

"I had not intended to love him; the reader knows I had wrought hard to extirpate from my soul the germs of love there detected; and now, at the first renewed view of him, they spontaneously revived, great and strong! He made me love him without looking at me."
— Charlotte Brontë, Jane Eyre

339

"This is not a goodbye, my darling, this is a thank you. Thank you for coming into my life and giving me joy, thank you for loving me and receiving my love in return. Thank you for the memories I will cherish forever. But most of all, thank you for showing me that there will come a time when I can eventually let you go.
I love you, T."

— Nicholas Sparks, Message in a
Bottle

340
"What was love, really? Flowers,
chocolate, and poetry? Or was it
something else? Was it being able to
finish someone's jokes? Was it having
absolute faith that someone was
there at your back? Was it knowing
someone so well that they instantly
understood why you did the things
you did—and shared those same
beliefs?"
— Richelle Mead, Last Sacrifice

341
"I think we ought to live happily ever
after."
— Diana Wynne Jones, Howl's Moving
Castle

342

"Let yourself be drawn by the stronger pull of that which you truly love."
— Rumi

343

"You only need one man to love you. But him to love you free like a wildfire, crazy like the moon, always like tomorrow, sudden like an inhale and overcoming like the tides. Only one man and all of this."
— C. JoyBell C.

344

"The things we love destroy us every time, lad. Remember that."
— George R.R. Martin, A Game of Thrones

345

"I am weird, you are weird. Everyone in this world is weird. One day two people come together in mutual weirdness and fall in love."
— Dr. Seuss

346
"Don't leave a piece of jewelry at his house so you can go back and get it later; he may be with his real girlfriend."
— Amy Sedaris, I Like You: Hospitality Under the Influence

347
"I know that the whole point—the only point—is to
find the things that matter, and hold on to them, and fight for them, and refuse to
let them go."
— Lauren Oliver, Delirium

348

"I want to try making things right because picking up the pieces is way better than leaving them the way they are."
— Simone Elkeles, Perfect Chemistry

349

"Never close your lips to those whom you have already opened your heart."
— Charles Dickens

350

"Throw your dreams into space like a kite, and you do not know what it will bring back, a new life, a new friend, a new love, a new country."
— Anaïs Nin

 351

"I wondered what happened when you offered yourself to someone, and they opened you, only to discover you were not the gift they expected and they had to smile and nod and say thank you all the same."
— Jodi Picoult, My Sister's Keeper

352

"In desperate love, we always invent the characters of our partners, demanding they be what we need of them, and then feeling devastated when they refuse to perform the role we created in the first place."
— Elizabeth Gilbert, Eat, Pray, Love

353

"If someone thinks that peace and love are just a cliche that must have been left behind in the 60s, that's a problem. Peace and love are eternal."

— John Lennon

354 ⚹
"My dear,
Find what you love and let it kill you.
Let it drain you of your all. Let it cling
onto your back and weigh you down
into eventual nothingness.
Let it kill you and let it devour your
remains.
For all things will kill you, both slowly
and fastly, but it's much better to be
killed by a lover.
~ Falsely yours"
— Charles Bukowski

355
"When you love someone you let
them take care of you."
— Jodi Picoult

356

"The love that moves the sun and the other stars."
— Elizabeth Gilbert

357
"Let me die the moment my love dies. Let me not outlive my own capacity to love.
Let me die still loving, and so, never die."
— Mary Zimmerman, Metamorphoses

358
"In the moment when I truly understand my enemy, understand him well enough to defeat him, then in that very moment I also love him. I think it's impossible to really understand somebody, what they want, what they believe, and not love them the way they love themselves.

And then, in that very moment when I love them.... I destroy them."
— Orson Scott Card, Ender's Game

359
"Don't waste your love on somebody, who doesn't value it."
— William Shakespeare, Romeo and Juliet

360
"It is the time you have wasted for your rose that makes your rose so important."
— Antoine de Saint-Exupéry, The Little Prince

361
"Yes, I decided, a man can truly change. The events of the past year have taught me much about myself, and a few universal truths. I learned,

for instance, that while wounds can be inflicted easily upon those we love, it's often much more difficult to heal them. Yet the process of healing those wounds provided the richest experience of my life, leading me to believe that while I've often overestimated what I could accomplish in a day, I had underestimated what I could do in a year. But most of all, I learned that it's possible for two people to fall in love all over again, even when there's been a lifetime of disappointment between them."
— Nicholas Sparks, The Wedding

362
"Love and compassion are necessities, not luxuries. Without them, humanity cannot survive."

— Dalai Lama XIV, The Art of Happiness

363

"It's so curious: one can resist tears and 'behave' very well in the hardest hours of grief. But then someone makes you a friendly sign behind a window, or one notices that a flower that was in bud only yesterday has suddenly blossomed, or a letter slips from a drawer... and everything collapses. "
— Colette

364

"I met an old lady once, almost a hundred years old, and she told me, 'There are only two questions that human beings have ever fought over, all through history. How much do you love me? And Who's in charge?"

— Elizabeth Gilbert, Eat, Pray, Love

365
"The day the power of love overrules the love of power, the world will know peace."
— Mahatma Gandhi

Also by Daniel Willey:

365 Fun, Uplifting, Motivating, and Inspirational Quotes You've Never Heard Before

365 Fun, Uplifting, and Inspirational Quotes from all the Top Movies

Be Great: 365 Inspirational Quotes from the World's Most Influential People

Success Isn't For Everyone: How to Build the Foundation for a Successful Future

The Top 365 Fun, Uplifting, Motivating, and Inspirational Quotes of all Time

About The Author

Daniel Willey became interested in books at a very young age. His mother was a huge advocate of reading and would regularly hold 'read-a-thons' for the family. Daniel graduated from the University of Utah in Emergency Medicine. He spent two years as a missionary in Thailand and has a great love for the country and people there. Daniel is currently writing another book and says that he has several ideas for more books "in the pipeline."